T0006664

A YEAR OF GOOD NEWS

BOXER BOOKS Ltd. and the distinctive Boxer Books logo are trademarks of Union Square & Co., LLC.
Union Square & Co., LLC, is a subsidiary of Sterling Publishing Co., Inc.
Text and illustrations © 2021 Martin Smatana
English translation © 2021 Julia and Peter Sherwood
Concept © 2021 Monokel, s.r.o.

All rights reserved. No part of this publication may be reproduced, stored in a retrieval system,
or transmitted in any form or by any means (including electronic, mechanical, photocopying,
recording, or otherwise) without prior written permission from the publisher.

All third-party trademarks, names, logos, and designs ("Trademarks") referenced herein are the property
of their respective owners. Unless specifically identified as such, use herein of any third-party trademarks
does not indicate any relationship, sponsorship, or endorsement between the author, the publisher, and
the trademark owner.

ISBN 978-1-914912-49-8

Library of Congress Control Number: 2022944015

For information about custom editions, special sales, and premium purchases,
please contact specialsales@unionsquareandco.com.

Printed in China

Lot #:
10 9 8 7 6 5 4 3 2 1

12/22

unionsquareandco.com

A YEAR OF GOOD NEWS

Martin Smatana

Boxer Books

I have always loved positive stories: whether in books I read as a child, or films I made as a grown-up, but above all in real life. During the pandemic, I began to feel that doom and gloom and bad news had taken over the world. I decided not to be beaten by this and set out to look for some good news.

I discovered that there is good news everywhere, from the end of our street to far away across the globe. Lots of good things happen every day, but they end up buried under "big" events. I decided to put good news under the spotlight and retell the stories in my own way.

I'm not very good at drawing, but I do make films with textiles. Using inspiration from my film *The Kite*, I decided to use old bits of thrown-away clothing to make models to show good news.

Initially I just made the occasional image for close friends. But when I saw how these stories lifted their spirits, I decided to cheer them up with an illustrated good news story every week.

Now, after a year's work, I would like to share the good news with you, too. This book consists of 52 good news stories from around the world. Some go further back in time, others are more recent than the "pandemic year," 2020. If any of the stories catch your imagination, the QR code at the end of the book will take you to the original news source where you can find out more.

Happy reading, everyone!

M. S.

1.

A refuse collector in Bogota, Colombia, collected
more than 25,000 books that people had thrown out,
and he now runs a public library for children in need
on the ground floor of his house.

2.

In a hospital in Valenciennes, France, children drive themselves to the operating room in electronic toy cars to help reduce their stress and fear of surgery.

3.

The director of a zoo in New South Wales,
Australia, brought home several red pandas,
saving them from a blazing bush fire.

4.

When an 85-year-old grandmother told her grandson
that she'd never seen the ocean or mountains, he took
her traveling all over the United States. They covered
40,000 miles (approximately 64,000 kilometers)
and visited 61 national parks.

5.

When flights from Palermo, Italy, were canceled due to the pandemic, a 10-year-old boy set out on foot with his father to visit his grandmother in London. They were joyfully reunited after 1,675 miles (2,700 kilometers) and 93 days, and two weeks in quarantine.

6.

A 22-year-old student with disabilities dreamed of climbing Mount Olympus. Her dream came true when an endurance runner carried her to Greece's highest peak in a specially modified backpack.

7.

When public events were canceled in Barcelona, Spain, a string quartet performed Puccini's *Chrysanthemums* at the local opera house in front of an audience of 2,292 houseplants. These were later given to healthcare workers to show gratitude for fighting the pandemic.

8.

Window cleaners in Kingston, Canada, dressed
as superheroes to cheer up patients in a children's
hospital. Iron Man, the Hulk, Spider-Man, and Batman
tackled dirty windows instead of crime.

9.

A Japanese woman who couldn't find a game she liked on her smartphone took up programming at the age of 81. After studying for three years, she designed a game inspired by traditional puppet theater. It has since been downloaded by tens of thousands of users.

10.

Hotels in San Francisco, California, forced to close because of the pandemic lit up their windows in the shape of a heart to give hope to people in challenging times.

11.

A professional cyclist in Italy delivered medicines and food to his pandemic-affected hometown in appreciation for the local support of him during the sports season.

12.

Firefighters in Utah cheered up a little
girl who was terrified after being in a car
crash by letting her paint their fingernails.

13.

When the closure of borders prevented
an 85-year-old German woman and an 89-year-old
Danish man from visiting each other, they found
a spot where only a single barrier divided the two
countries. There they met every day, sitting at
a folding table, chatting and surprising each
other with small gifts.

14.

A 109-year-old man in Australia knitted
wool sweaters for penguins threatened by
an oil leak to stop them from swallowing the
toxic oil while cleaning themselves.

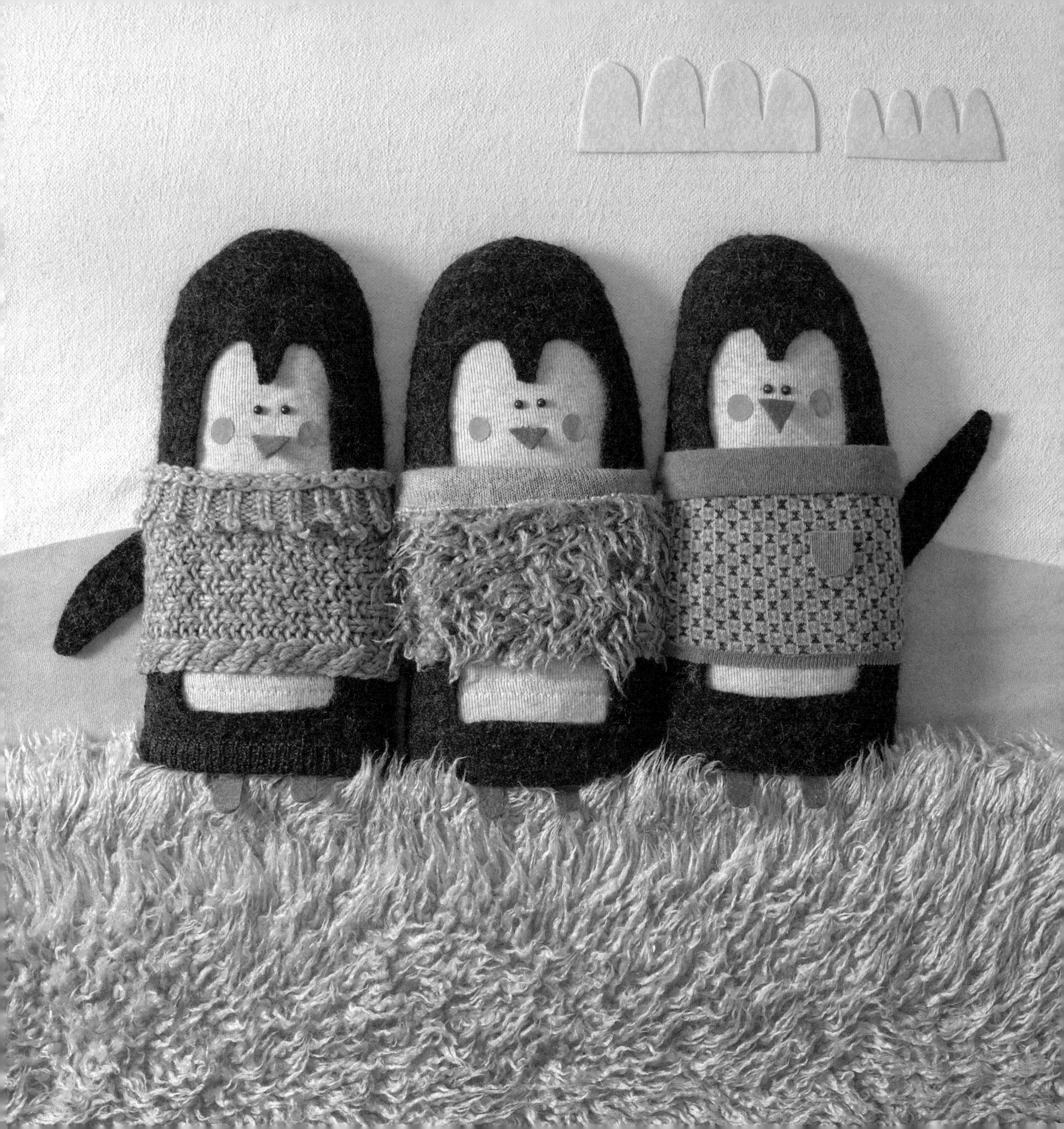

15.

To lift the spirits of their neighbors,
a family in Somerset, England, painted their
house in cheerful colors, brick by brick.

16.

A father who wanted to spend Christmas with his
flight attendant daughter bought tickets for all six flights
she worked on during the holiday season.

17.

People confined to their homes during lockdown
clapped, blew air horns, and banged pots and pans
every evening to thank frontline workers—
healthcare staff, firefighters, and store workers.

18.

The authorities in Iceland recommended that lonely people missing physical contact during the pandemic hug trees. Research has shown that this is very beneficial, reducing stress and improving general health.

19.

A Czech artist in Austria built birdhouses for
a retirement home that looked like the residents'
own former houses so that they would be
surrounded by things that formed part of
their own memories.

20.

When a bookshop in the Slovak town
of Žilina was forced to close during the
pandemic, the booksellers distributed books
to their readers on bikes and scooters.

21.

After his flights were canceled, a man spent 85 days
sailing across the Atlantic from Portugal to Argentina
to get there in time for his father's 90th birthday.

22.

In order to spend more time with his
10 grandchildren, a proud grandfather
in Oregon bought a decommissioned
school bus and started driving them
to school in the mornings.

23.

In Italy, a healthcare worker in a protective
suit surprised an 86-year-old hospital patient
by asking her to dance. The entire floor
cheered them on as they waltzed.

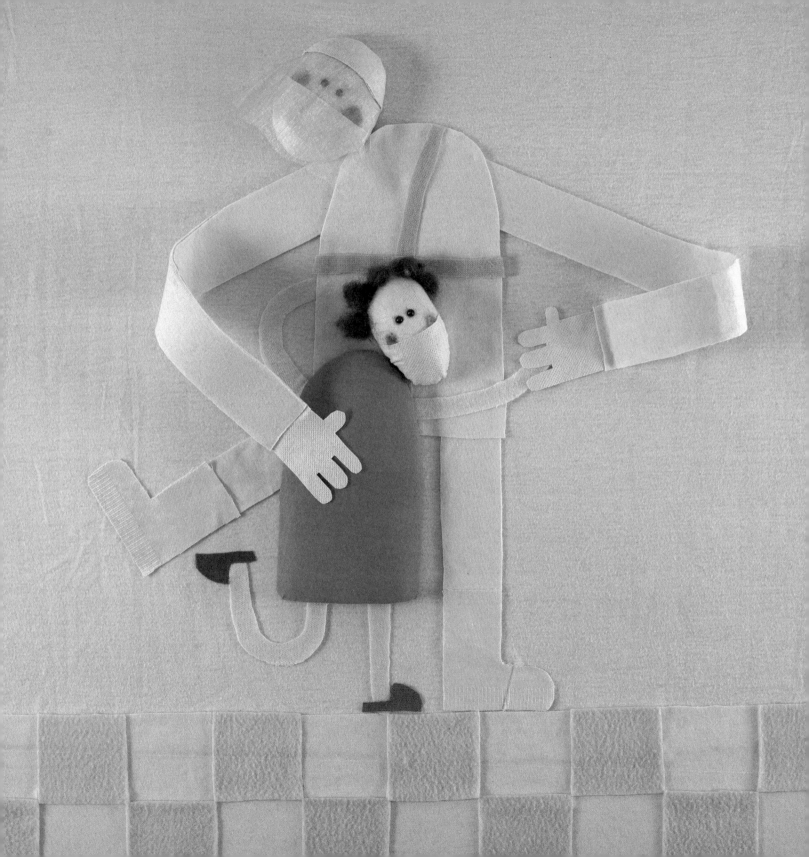

24.

Australian firefighters dropped tons
of fruit and vegetables from helicopters to
the scorched earth to feed starving animals
as devastating wildfires raged.

25.

When the border between Český Těšín, Czech
Republic, and the neighboring Polish city of Cieszyn
was closed during the pandemic, residents of the two
cities exchanged messages across the river to tell
their neighbors how much they missed them.

Czech (right side) I MISS YOU
Polish (left side) I MISS YOU, TOO

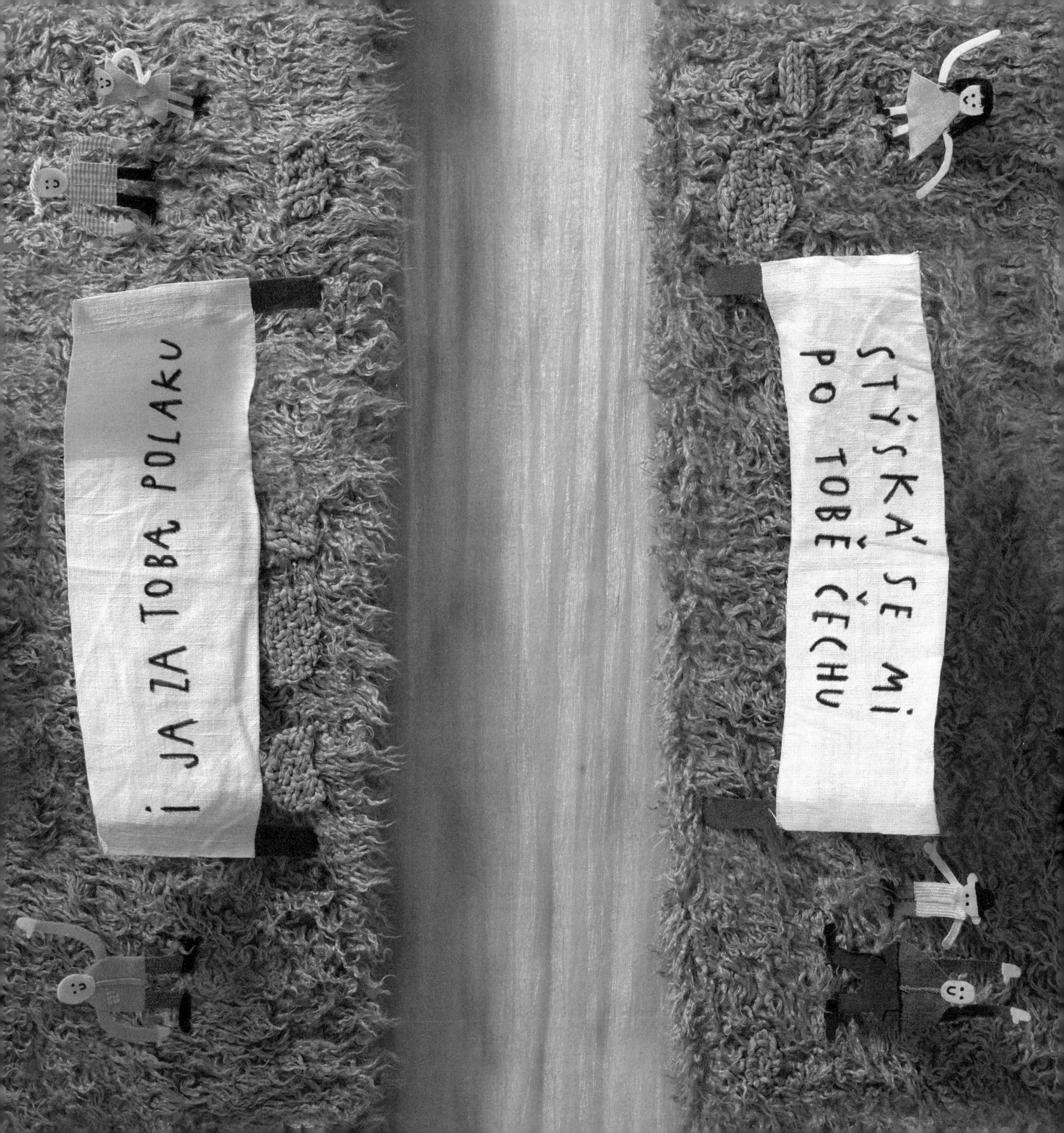

STÝSKÁ SE MI
PO TOBĚ ČECHU
I JA ZA TOBĄ POLAKU

26.

A Chinese farmer traveled on a motorbike
for 24 years, covering 300,000 miles, until he
found his son, who had been kidnapped by
gunmen as a young boy.

27.

When students in Bristol, England,
learned that their school's caretaker hadn't visited
his relatives in his native Jamaica for four years,
they collected money for his plane ticket.

28.

To give back to nature what it has taken from it,
a Danish company has invented pencils that can be
planted after use so that they grow into an herb,
a shrub, or a tree.

29.

Listening to a recording of music from *Swan Lake*, a once-famous Spanish prima ballerina suffering from Alzheimer's disease recalled the choreography and started to dance.

30.

For the second time in history, an international
team of refugees took part in the 2020 Tokyo Olympics.
Twenty-nine athletes forced to flee their homes because of
war or oppression competed together under a joint flag.

31.

Italian healthcare workers had images of their smiling faces printed on their protective suits to humanize the antiseptic space of the hospital and show patients that they were not alone.

32.

To stop children from feeling lonely while waiting
for a bus, their grandparents made a life-size statue
of the famous Japanese character Totoro and installed
it at the bus stop.

33.

In Italian cities, people played music and sang
from their windows during lockdown to cheer
up their neighbors and show solidarity.

34.

To bring some nature into the cities and help honeybees, flowers were planted on the roofs of bus stop shelters in the Netherlands.

35.

During lockdown, the Canadian post office
sent every household in the country postcards
with messages of gratitude and solidarity.
People could add their own words and send the
cards to their loved ones free of charge to
keep in touch during the pandemic.

36.

Friendship knows no bounds, as children
in the United States and Mexico proved by
playing on a seesaw together—each on their
side of the closely guarded border.

37.

Shortly before his 100th birthday, a British war veteran
pledged to cross his backyard one hundred times with his
walker to raise money for the National Health Service.
After raising 32 million pounds (38 million dollars),
he was knighted by Queen Elizabeth II.

38.

For the past 130 years, people in love have been
mailing letters in a hollow tree in Eutin, Germany.
The tree, which now has its own postal address,
has brought thousands of people together in
friendship, and some even in marriage.

39.

A man in the Miyazaki prefecture in Japan
spent two years planting flowers for his blind
wife so that she could enjoy the garden
through its fragrance.

40.

In the town of Zermatt, people showed
their solidarity with countries badly hit by the
pandemic by projecting their national flags
onto Switzerland's highest peak.

41.

A well-known Swedish furniture maker
published illustrated instructions showing
children how to build a bunker, a castle,
or a tent at home, helping many families get
through the difficult times of self-isolation
and closed schools.

42.

People in Denmark and some other
European countries can rent kayaks free
of charge provided they agree to pick up litter
while paddling down the waterways.

43.

After decades-long efforts, polio has been eradicated
in Africa. Vaccination has saved an estimated 1.8 million
children from being paralyzed for life and prevented
180,000 deaths.

44.

Residents of a French retirement home
have been developing their motor and creative
skills in a variety of ways—for example, by taking
courses in electronic and techno music.

45.

Children who were stuck at home for months on end during the pandemic drew pictures of rainbows and put them up in their windows to cheer up their neighbors and spread hope.

46.

A store worker in Pardubice, Czech Republic,
went to the police to hand in an envelope full of money
left by a customer and would not accept a finder's fee.
A Czech brewery gave him a year's supply of beer that people
can buy in his store for a voluntary donation, which
he uses to help children with disabilities.

47.

After a year of distance learning, teachers in Spain
decided to move classes to the local beach. The children
were socially distanced and in the fresh air, and the
teachers used their proximity to the sea and islands
to give lessons in biology and geography.

48.

Many families adopted dogs during lockdown,
leaving dog shelters almost empty. Lonely people in
particular appreciated animal companionship, which
helped them overcome their fear of the pandemic
and made them feel safer.

49.

Orphaned children in Montreal, Canada, have been making daily visits to retirement homes, spending time with the residents and benefiting from cross-generational learning.

50.

A French florist left bright bunches
of flowers on cars parked outside
a hospital to thank healthcare workers.

51.

When the 11-day war between Israel
and Palestine ended, an Israeli nursery school
teacher donated a kidney to a 3-year-old
boy from the Gaza Strip.

52.

For many years, an elderly lady in Comox, Canada,
used to wave to students on their way to school.
The day she was due to move to a retirement home,
hundreds of students gathered outside her
house to say good-bye.

Every day good-news stories like these
get buried in the barrage of bad news.
Let us keep an eye out for them in the
media and in our immediate surroundings.
The world is a much better place to live
in than it often seems.

If you would like to know more about these good news stories, please scan this QR code.

www.yearofgoodnews.com

I would like to thank everyone who has helped me with this project: Peter Michalík, Františka Benčaťová, Veronika Zacharová, Ondřej Nedvěd, Dominik Prokop, Elizabeth Bugyiová, Martina Figusch Rozinajová, Zuzana Čupová, Zuzana A. Ferusová, Marek Adamov, Denisa Ballová, Ema Benčaťová, Tamara Bračová, Pavlína Černá, Tomáš Danay, Samuel Gabura, Altin Gashi, Simona Gottierová, Marek Jančúch, Marek Ježo, Katka Končová, Monika Konopásková, Simona Koutná, Katarína Krištúfková, Veronika Michalíková, Michaela Paštéková, Saša Petrášová, Renáta Rábeková, Martina Rusnáková, Miroslav Smatana, Veronika Suchovská, Ivan Zaťko, and others.

I am also grateful to the New Synagogue in Žilina for providing the space and great atmosphere for working on the first illustrations; and to the Blue Faces studio for the space and technical support in completing the project.

Last but not least, many thanks to Simonka for a year full of lovely moments.